The Crystal Ou

Alison Fell was born in Dumfries, Scotland in 1944 and raised in villages in the Highlands and the Borders. In 1969 she co-founded the radical theatre group Welfare State and in 1970 moved to London to work in the Women's Street Theatre Group and later on *Spare Rib*. Currently she runs writers' workshops in London. Her poetry has been published in several anthologies, amongst them *Smile Smile Smile Smile*, *One Foot on the Mountain*, *Bread and Roses* (Virago, 1982), *Angels of Fire* (Chatto & Windus), *Apples and Snakes* (Pluto Press, 1985) and in a first individual collection *Kisses for Mayakovsky* (Virago, 1984) which won the Alice Hunt Bartlett Award for poetry in 1984. Her work was also included in the 'Britain Salutes New York' Festival in 1984, in the nationwide Poetry Live Festival in the UK in 1987, and is featured in an issue of *Partisan Review* focussing on British poetry. She has read widely at events and venues throughout the UK, including the Institute of Contemporary Arts, the Queen Elizabeth Hall and the Assembly Rooms, Edinburgh. In 1981 her children's novel *The Grey Dancer* was published by Collins. *Every Move You Make*, a political novel set among the urban activists of the seventies, was published by Virago in 1984, and *The Bad Box*, a novel about adolescence in the Scotland of the late fifties and early sixties, was published in 1987.

Also by Alison Fell

Poetry
Kisses for Mayakovsky

Novels
Every Move You Make
The Bad Box

Novels for children
The Grey Dancer

Alison Fell

THE CRYSTAL OWL

A Methuen Paperback

A Methuen Paperback

THE CRYSTAL OWL

British Library Cataloguing in Publication Data
Fell, Alison
  The crystal owl.
  I. Title
  821′.914

  ISBN 0-413-18810-8

First published in Great Britain 1988
by Methuen London
81 Fulham Road, London SW3 6RB
Copyright © 1988 by Alison Fell
Photoset by Rowland Phototypesetting Ltd
Bury St Edmunds, Suffolk
Printed and bound in Great Britain
by Cox and Wyman Ltd, Reading, Berks.

Contents

The Mistresses   7
The Blue Angel   8
Alphaville and after   9
the heat of the moment   11
A day like a hotel   14
sorority   15
Medusa   16
Medusa on Skyros   17
Summer love poems   18
   1. Heat waves   18
   2. All you have to do   20
The Skating Lesson   21
The long goodbye   22
Cornfield with skylark   23
Liberating Dachau   25
Bourj-al-Barajneh   27
Freeze-frame   29
The crystal owl   31
Parks, encounters, alarms   33
   1. Pigeons   33
   2. Hotel Molière   35
   3. the other woman living in her teeth   36
   4. heart-breaker   37
the words to say it   38
Putting on the Ritz   39
Cassandra flies Olympic   41
when the music changes   42
Untitled   44
Aphonia   45
Kalimera   46
Hallowe'en Dreams   48
Scapegoat   50

Mammy Said   52
The Rothko room, Tate Gallery   54
My father's plane   56
in proportion   57
Fille de joie   59
postscriptcard   60
accidents of deterioration in which passages
    are destroyed by rewinding   61
The Sailor from Gibraltar   62
Naturally   64
Rodin's Muse   66
Jazzsongs for Gina   68
    1. Moongirls – a Round   68
    2. Louis Bird   69
    3. November   70
For Ann, returning   71
'A tender youth without fault or blemish'   72
Fantasia for Mary Wollstonecraft   74
Interlude – the windmill   80
The single woman considers herself   81
Below the Ecrins   82
Photographs of the Alps seen from New South Wales   84
who's been sleeping in *my* bed?   88
Rune   89

The Mistresses

While our lovers were in London with their wives,
L. and I spent Christmas in Wales caretaking a
friend's house and animals. We wrote, L. raged
regularly, I worked on a relationship with the
head goat. There were many starry frosts. . . .

Welsh winter: jealous goats
butt to be petted. Long white
cat on my shoulder. Grey dog
with its colonel's eyebrows
hogging the fire. Outside, bantams
to keep from the Christmas fox,
and rabbits aureoled in the torchlight.

You're in the woodshed, mossy-haired
and murdering logs. Your rages
are diurnal, like coast winds
or the rite of milking. Sun-up
and moonrise, these are dead
lovers' limbs in your wheelbarrow.

I appeal to the mirror
and your intelligence. Look
at the silk and size of us,
our fleece and unction.
See how we burn, not wives
but mud witches kneading
the hot udder of the goat,
our laughter glittering
over the white spirit, while
stars pepper our night heads,
and the memories of our loves
festoon us like warm animals

The Blue Angel

Wales also, and the power of the moon to summon up longings which seemed to be safely packed away. In the film of the same name, Marlene Dietrich plays temptress to the older professor. Except in this poem the roles – and ages – are reversed.

Bright moonlight woke me like a cheat
My face offered itself
My arms were tricked open
when I had been curled tight
around forgetting

Sometimes in the night
I woke to find you watching
You curved over me like a harp
Your pale stare was on me

The moon gloats
The moon sucks me up
like a blown egg
I think you must live there
hoarding all I have

My eyes are full of thistles
and mustard
If only you hadn't entered my sleep
deep as a dawn bird enters
You bright cheating moonlight
You blue angel

Alphaville and after

we never did
   get to Paris
   but yes
   in Usclas
the days opened
like blue shutters
on fictions of other cities

   a bed
   wide as the sea
   the pomegranate
that Persephone-tree,
like a fire in the field

these minutes
   we were married to
   nights
in the underworld
   believing
   we ate people
   possibly
we were gods

just another love poem
   your fruit
   mine
   the light
seeded in our thighs

   unstable bargains
which end like Alphaville:
   Paris snowbound
under a swaying bare light-bulb
   words of love
   reflections of night trains
   nowhere to go

the heat of the moment

Leewark, Johannesburg, 1985. Two Afrikaners
are tried for the murder of a black girl,
found guilty, and sentenced to death.
White South Africa reels at this turn of the
tide. But then, what fascists of all countries
share is a vision of themselves as chosen
people whom God ought therefore to exempt from
all suffering. *Ag Here* is Afrikaans for
For God's sake.

crossing the city where nowhere
resembles us, the moon
is schizoid and unkind,
the NF men on the tube
hold their white balls,
fucking and blinding:
if they burst it will be all our fault

there is silence
and there is
what can be said

a jet-ride away,
not far from Johannesburg,
listen and you will hear
the shreds of the white melody

it was only rape, Ag Here,
crime of light hearts
and the ebullience of boys

black girl 19 burns in a locked car boot
a girl burning like a forest

the sky has no right
to its magic, the night
to its bright bones

the townspeople have demanded
nothing less than the death penalty

listen hard, the hands say,
turn the words over and around like stones

look
at the arrows in our eye,
the brittle ring our shoulders make
around the blue morning

know too
that hell is here
at the blunt end of a bulldozed road
in an invented country

dogs pant in chorus
under a bad red sun

relatives of the accused were reported
to be in a state of shock
relatives of the accused were supported
from the courtroom in a state of collapse

the suffering of the arrogant
is always ugly
it is livid and exiled, a goblin rage
twists under its lardy tears

let pain be elsewhere
let them carry it for us like cordial
let it knot odd boots with copper wire
let its hair turn grey on its neck like snow
let its birthright be burning,
a shadowed dark wood to light
our white hearths, our white faces

A day like a hotel

(for G.)

In the next room
you light
another cigarette:

blue gauloises
for your earth-
dreams. It's morning,

the wallpaper hour; the house
breathes at your back,
foreign

and pale. Already
you have counted
all you own

as if
you were leaving.
On a day which withholds

pain and pleasure,
your corridors
are polished

to exhaustion,
your blank shoes challenge
in a row

sorority

we are here
we work quietly
in empty rooms

we stroke
the spokes of the poem

it is the dream
it is the new blue dress
we want to keep secret
yet wear in the open

it is the guest
at the threshold
the host
waiting stretched
and delicate as a parasol

from light
or from darkness
someone who loves us
is coming
hurrying
over the hungry world

Medusa

An Etruscan head, two-sided, one sweetly blank
and appealing, the other a Medusa, a she-devil.
It was easy enough to live out this dichotomy
on the page, to enter the anger and vengefulness.
I was also taken with the idea that this Medusa
only makes manifest what is already there –
the deep obdurate withholding which enrages her.

Once I was smooth
as saints, ceramic-faced;
my smile glanced, my hair
fell meekly. From my thighs
men mounted planets.

Now in a halo of snakes
I am basalt
I bare my black brows,
my greedy pelican jaw
wide-stretched for bones
and grinding.

It's no riddle, who
raddled me.

Swivel if my fish eye
is on you,
for I am your mirror
and I see you deeply,
down to the stone,
to the plain truth of it

Medusa on Skyros

A flesh and blood Medusa, witty and brave
in the midst of narcissistic tourist youth . . .

in the parading square
  where glossed nations
    muddle
      in their young
    Eurotans
  a woman
whose bruised face
  bags
    and bounces
      when she laughs
    raises
  her bright brown
wig
  to the men
    of middling age
  who have been flirting
cool and kingly
  into her eyes
    into the deep stretched silk
      of her breasts
    and oh
  they go
ghostly –
  ai! ai!
    in the rattle
      of all the small
    ouzo bottles
  as she flaunts
their sudden skulls
  grinning
    in the bristle
      of her short grey hair

Summer love poems

1. Heat waves

On a burning North London Line platform,
feeling sticky, earthbound, female.
All the more so since I'm thinking of an
American friend climbing perilous cliffs
in Cornwall. His postcards are confident,
buoyant. At the end of the week, he says,
they'll go to Anglesey to climb
a long, exposed face called 'A Dream of
White Horses'.

90 degrees. So noon and furious.
Me. Waiting for a train.
Waiting. Getting empty. Tongue
cracking up from sucking my
teeth. Men circling me
as in my mind I circle you:
I keep my weather eye open.
200 miles away there may be
chalk falls in the clear
afternoon where you are,
high up, leaning away
from the clean edge
of your hot shadow.
Paying out the rope.

Dogs barking somewhere. A French
boy sighs to his book: *'orage de
ses désespoirs'*. The windows
of the city are thrown wide.

You. Skirting the meaning of
the sea, white wool of your
mother's arms and the underneath
bleed of your dreams.

Me. Riding the long snake
of my life. Diesel and soot. Doors
closing and opening.

2. *All you have to do*

A river bank in the Hérault district of France.
Fishermen, youths playing and swimming.
The same American friend having difficulty,
as men will, with his feelings.

Somehow these wading ordinary
boys beating the water lightly
are eating your heart out

I say their hands are like dragonflies
I say the space between fingers
and river is a measure of love

Meanwhile you're holding a knifeblade
loose as a flower but pointing up

Itching, you say, for your calf,
blood, some nerve in your emptiness

Eyes narrowly bitching at me
as if I'm too hot and bright.

I say you're playing dead, wanting
Vietnam or someone to blame

I say you can break cover, just
come without maps and calling
my name. All you have to do

Is ask. We'll pet the thin
summer black of the night, keeping
the sun back, and my love
will spin you in

The Skating Lesson

Oh what a hopeless tousle. He wants her,
but he also wants his marriage back with
a great howling need. The future is opaque,
for neither of them can bear to look the end
in the eye. And so, knowing that she should
know better, she does gymnastics with her self.

After all this time he is going home
with his hope like a hammer
and his unfinished eyes,
but first he is teaching you
frost and balance.

(No need to lie, under
the red skirt of summer
we were liquid and mad,
orchards to each other –
how will he explain this away?)

Cold-nosed he is dancing backwards,
holding out his arms.
(His scissor-spin and snap,
his Hey Lady grin
and his heart bolting)

Make no mistakes
Don't tax him
Listen to the organ's
chronic electric song.
The light on the ice is wet.
Don't look into it. Think dry.
Below you the blades grey
as fish teeth and harsh.
Push right. Push left.
You love. You move, you move.

The long goodbye

In the dim light
something has broken

you wear a stripe
of white pain like a badger
and I can't say why I'm crying

except that the tunnel of this room
is long as your marriage

except that I have dreamed you
overhead like a fairground or
bright teeming plane

this goodbye has wormed
and bred in the dark
under my breasts

I see you touch her comfortably,
lip to lip

feel now in stillness
how our shadows lose
the measure of each other

Cornfield with skylark

On 30 March 1987, with gross pomp
and circumstance, Van Gogh's
'Sunflowers' were sold at Sotheby's
for 22½ million pounds plus commission.

Close up. Coins
stirred in the wet
of a café table

luminously, a blotched
letter:
My dear generous Theo

Long shot. The North
Sea shouldering
at sluice-gates:

Holland, where windows
measure wealth
and the sun

is thin as scorn. Perhaps
it is as his father
said

all
he accumulates
is lack

(the black eyes
of the cornflower
stars, roar

of the sun in his head,
the sinless sky
circling the bright

wheat,
the church tower tortured
or rejoicing)

Close up. Coins,
a letter:
this one for blood-

money, this
for the magpies

with their stolen
bitter news

(fallen
cherry-blossom, the gutters
are steep screes of it)

Liberating Dachau

May 1985 brought the anniversary of Victory in Europe
to the television screen. An American cameraman who
accompanied his unit into Dachau watches the footage
he shot forty years ago, and searches for words,
even now weeping, struggling to comprehend, shaking
his head again and again.

Impossible to even think of,
the cameraman says, with that

bald freeze of dolls at the back
of his eyes. He says they had been

gnawing at themselves, and possibly
at each other. He says the snow

shrouded them, stroked them like fox
fur, their caved chests, their hopeless

pajamas. (Poles, Byelorussians, the odd
Communist. One was a bad barber, one

a mender of clocks, one broke women
like bright leaves)

They hang now, they are braced
and shrunk, the dimensions

drawn out of them. (The trance,
the tale, the white stir of water,

the wheel of sparks.) Impossible
to even think of such robbery.

The blanched dead are boxed
in the mirrors of their eyes

Their hair fritters to light
nets in the mackerel sky

Their hair falls from the still
firs to enter our mouths

Bourj-al-Barajneh

In the winter of 1986–87, Bourj-al-Barajneh, a Palestinian
camp on the outskirts of Beirut, was besieged by Shi-ite
Amal militiamen for five months. The refugees ate cats, dogs
and rats to stay alive. Women and children ran the blockade
of gunfire to fetch in small amounts of food, but the
militia were not selective in their targeting. There were
many casualties, until the Syrian army finally relieved the
camp on 6 April 1987.

   Earlier, a British television journalist who had penetrated
the camp sent back film footage of twelve-year-old girls running
the 'Corridor of Death'.

Down the green gulley
she bounces, a terrible rabbit
in her brother's clothes.
Stained pale by the moon
and hunger,
she runs on curses:

mother forgive me
the white belly of my death
rears up secretly
in the night   how red
the prod of the crossfire
I keep to the corners
of my eyes

your hand   flicks
like a tongue
from the thin alley
fifty yards on
in that torn warren
the wind tinkers with

for love of the dead
you will give me a cigarette
I will suck sideways
with all of my mouth

the wild wind takes me
by the hand
mother of many colours
is its name
it is blameless   knows
no malice   does not
fear for me   I cannot help
loving it   I cannot help
loving

Freeze-frame

On my bedroom wall there's an old black-and-white snapshot
of two sisters in a snow-crusted garden. The wee one is
caught in the act of smashing a snowball at the big one,
who stands knock-kneed, unprotesting.

1947. That winter they talk of.
A winter like fists or wizards,

one or the other. The frozen lawn
pitted with porridge and scraps,

soup-bone fat with marrow
that the crows brawl over,

big sister buttoned up
with her puppet gloves dangling.

For background, there's the gable
where old Jessie lived,

a black wedge, and her
the witch of a hundred cats,

reading
your mind's eye, your bad eye.

1947. Small birds dumb as dolls
on the winter wire. I saw

their hearts like peas
and pitied them

that they were never born with tongues
to tell us things. I emptied

my wishes up chimneys, insisted
on reindeer.

Click of the camera fixes
my mittened hand to a blur:

the snowball's invisible as anger
shuttered in the nick of time.

My sister is too patient,
with her face like Petrouchka

and her snow-drifted smile.
She has no tongue, she says

nothing, thinks of Jessie
with the soot under her skirts

and the cats
wicked on the wall

The crystal owl

Almost forty years on from the photograph,
and after a separation of eighteen years,
I visited my sister in Tasmania. We looked
back at our childhood, collaborators,
each needing the other to be her witness.
Yes, we said, shivering with relief, it
was so, it was like that. We even laughed
at the roles which had been assigned
to us – the placid one, the highly strung
one. Yet with every moment we were marking
out boundaries, differentiating each
other. I itched for her to demand more,
get her teeth into life; she found me
too thin and frenetic and citified.
Tremendous tenderness and irritation. . . .

An ancient fridge
hums at the heart
of my sister's house.
Dead
hydrangea heads
bludgeon the high window.

Still as an island, she sits
in profusion,
watching the wattle-leaves
wither at the door,
the mourning march of bottles
across the kitchen corners.

She who can sever nothing,
shrinks
from that kookaburra
scissoring up a snake,
while I
with my secateurs
scurry to make order.

The big woman nods
in the balcony monotony,
living scarce in the air
like a breath:

I am her long knife,
her thief,
the crystal owl which flurries
in the facets of her eyes.

She is the slowest pulse,
the rule
of water; with relief
she lets the surface
slither over.

Look at the child now,
who courts herself in dreams,
who sleeps lit up
like a pumpkin.
Look at the smile, spell-
bound and freed.

In her dreams she has
eight crystal claws to catch
that kiss
I ran after her to deliver.

Butter-and-sugar her,
wrap her in blue bonnets,
Take her to the forest
to try for paradise

Parks, encounters, alarms

*Does it stitch, says the German girl at the swimming pond,
meaning, does it sting, meaning a dragonfly skirting the
water's edge. I wait for it, but only inviting, thinking of
unseen tracks which even ego could interrupt. Or the brush
of my breaths, in and out. Ducks flicker past, and after half
an hour of advances, retreats, advances, the dragonfly
comes close, nose to nose and very interested. Its yellow
head most surprisingly shaped like railway buffer or
flattened bullet, its body a night train hanging in the air,
striped with lit windows and drawn blue blinds. Among the
wet nettles we consider each other, sheepish, blinking
awake, two transients in some midday station, wondering
what the word is for harmless . . .*

1.   *Pigeons*

Pigeons
are tossing up
seeds
and bread.
Their pecking is snappish,
they want
what they want
and the rest
goes in whirligigs
like salt over their shoulders.

Today
when I said
I was writing about you –
for women will make meat and bread
of their long tearings –
you looked like that puffed
angry one
in its purple ruff;
yes,
that's
what you looked like.

2. *Hotel Molière*

no tennis game ever made
me as sad   as that gay
galloping one I saw   in the
Luxembourg   that grey day
with the forsythia just
struggling out   the bedroom
so yellow, too   suggesting
high jinks and skittish breakfasts
and I thought – if only
you could see me dance –
but your small red mouth
stung your face   you ran out
to drink coffee   and the oysters
I ate to please you   had
no colour   and tasted of
cold draughts

3. *the other woman living in her teeth*

Seething and strategising over a bag of cherries

swimming pool subdued by hot
cloud moods blow willow-cotton
crowding the wind silly silly
how your silence stifles coot
cricks its neck cracks like walk-
ing sticks I know a thing or two
for instance absolutely the best
cherries aren't scarlet but dark
grinning red like pirates speckled
muscularly sour so I won't
call you sweetly I won't call
you sweet I won't call you

4. *heart-breaker*

wheelchair lady
approaching 100 years old
in white straw hat
with pink petunia
and fine angry eyes on me
because she too
was once long as a lily
and in love
because today
they tucked her disastrous limbs
neatly sideways
and dressed her for holidays
and she thinks I don't know
petunia was her colour
the one she stung
and blistered in
and she thinks I don't know
what laughter seamed
her quartz and cunning face
and she thinks I don't know
what's coming to me

the words to say it

in the night the words come down
dream peacocks strutting for dear life
in the noise of the field and the birds in it

trailing for mates, blue winds fan
their great tails
(their tails spreading dust and rainbows,
their insolent rant of happiness)

this is how, loving and speaking, we
quake, moon, embrace, until dawn
aches across the bed, ghosts
and colours are dumb
and morning makes me a
house of nonsense
stains of teabags
flat shadows burned into the walls
the telephone city tinkling to itself –

light, garrulous, how *are* you?

Putting on the Ritz

After fifteen years of friendship and rivalry in life
and writing, M. is leaving the country. We agree to
dress up, say farewell in fine style, our heads a jumble
of feminism and film noir, Simone de Beauvoir and
Bette Davis, our bodies, as always, wondering just who
we are. But honestly – the Ritz? Will our class-
consciousness ever tolerate it?

Before you take that plane
for America
you and me
we'll take tea at the Ritz,
literary ladies
with shoulders square as skyscrapers

In between waiters
you'll make a macaroon mouth
and tell me
Sometimes in marriage
you have to play at hamsters

And hooking my hand
in my hair
I'll meet envy the old gangster
just for a moment –

In our tango of books and babies
do I need to tell you
he'll be kissing us to the point
of no return?

There'll be pyramids of kumquats,
the dazzling Texan teeth
of chandeliers –

Did I ever mention
that the narrative mode of the era
was paranoia?

We'll see hard money
in the unswerving eyes,
a town, as Rilke said,
where nothing is forgiven –

Do I need to tell you
that we aren't just longing
but lucky?

That in our Cinderella shoes
we'll know ourselves
raggedy and rich

And when rapid rain comes
tappetting like Fred Astaire
we'll eke a bat-black umbrella
between us –

Do I need to tell you
we'll be chins to the wind
like all the best movies,

Steering the helms of our hats
by the skins of our teeth
to the getaway alley
where the dream-taxi
trembles, revving
its red engines

Cassandra flies Olympic

A poem dedicated to Olympic Airways, who, after an aborted
take-off at Heathrow, made us wait for eighteen hours while
they flew spare parts in from Paris (wings? engines?),
and then took off again for Athens in the same machine.

five miles high above Athens
something ancient
tells her she's in for it

this little fleeing ton of metal
fat as a brick
can clatter down the unsafe sky

some debris of birds or gods
ripping the jets apart, or else
the tailplane nipped off
by satellite peelings

if she could only cry oracular
along the blond coffin of faces
which talk rockabye
and beer
and living rooms

(we will fall off the edge
of a wall of wind
we will tumble back down
to the tossed thick sea
and the blue ships)

can't they see the collison
in her face
already like a robbed nest
chaotic with glue and shell shards and feathers?

when the music changes

A greek island, a roof-garden café looking out
over white cubist houses to the hills beyond.
In the downstairs bar, the handsome café-owner
plays Clapton, Springsteen: siren music to lure
in the golden girls.

the dutch girl settles
her black cigarette-lighter
exactly on the edge of the music

her sitting is a statement
which flowers
only in these chords, this
café table, the scoured dry blue
backdrop of mountains,

an emptiness into which
some something must,
she thinks,
come spiralling

won't you please
the waiting, the glamour
of the guitar crying out,
won't you please read my sign,
be a gypsy

the music does it, the magic
is all made for her:
the glass lie, the slipper
that fits
tell me what I want to find,
deep within me

when the music changes, a frown
will sting her face, for now
nothing speaks for her, only
her bare shoulders,
her black cigarette-lighter,
the thin thumb
lightly pecking her mouth

sun on the crown
of a straw hat.
the chair still in shade.
morning
moving into the room.

Aphonia

Separation confuses as much as it hurts,
as if loss disrupts some basic syntax,
as if the child, flailing, asks whose
fault?, and finds all answers insupportable.
    (*Aphonic*: voiceless or devoiced.)

Beyond tight shutters
the night
is all rut
and riot, a zoo
of hot noise
and I in it
unable to bark back,
for it's all
Greek to me –
the jumbled wind
baying in the fire escape,
the squeak of cockerels –
some impossible alphabet
of wounds now I've lost
the thread of you.
If only we hadn't made
such a good sentence,
but oh yes
we rang.
In the dumb sheets
I think of us
loving back to front
(that pure urgency like dogs)
and wonder:
is there anything
still
always
stringing us
together

Kalimera

Dawn sheep
  still as frost
    in a field
of empty melon skins.
    Kalimera, I say,
kalimera.

Tireless day
  glares
    into my corners.
On the windburned beach
  the jukebox grinds
agape mou:
  love me.
Sunhats howl
  across the sand.

I can't see you
  for colours,
    marble-vulgar:
the oleanders,
  brittle blue of sea,
    the pedalos'
  devastating red.

In the morning
  I see
    the cross on the church
      like a white butterfly,
yellow eyes
  of the café owner.
Kalimera, I say,
  kalimera.

All day long
  the colours
    topple into the sea.

Hallowe'en Dreams

Ten thousand jet-lagged miles to Australia,
and this time the separation is also an escape –
but the confusion remains. Dreams and nostalgia
move backwards; you catch the tail end and
burrow back to find the beginning – in this
case, all the way back to the Northern Hemisphere,
to Hammer films and childhood snippets of Burns,
and that seductive witch the Cutty Sark, who
tried to capture the fleeing Tam O'Shanter,
but only managed to snatch off his grey mare's tail.

In the beginning
    she escaped for foreign parts
        sad and sound
            suddenly
        an old lady
    Nijinsky had just blown away
        shredded to a feather
            in seconds –
        brief papery face
    the regular Dracula finale
after a fate Tam O'Shanter
    avoided narrowly
        halfway
            across the bridge
        seeming to lose her
    hand snatched by the Cutty Sark
(he could not cross water in any case)
    Once upon a time powerful
        she cowered back
            able to reduce men to rage
        in the half-dark
    saw his wildcat snarl

the red-and-white football scarf
   he took off
      at some point
         to strangle her with
      accusing her of desertion
   so furiously
that she was afraid
   yet he was the one
      she reminded him
         who had chosen to leave her
      (not conversely)
   when earlier he had kissed her
against a fencepost
   or some tree-trunk
      above a dark sea sullenly
         even punitively

Scapegoat

Summer and Chernobyl in Europe: topsy-turvy winter in safe
clean New Zealand. The womenfolk of the family – my mother,
sister and I – had a reunion after years apart. Under the jokes
and joyfulness there were currents of confusion and
ambivalence – but how were these checked, unspoken feelings
to surface?

in the house on the ridge
above the valley of apples
where Dutchmen shake out their golden hair

we are the daughters of delight
welcomed in our silver and better selves

we eat
sweet tea/wool/rings grinding as glass
our scones in the oven are chubby as cupids

mother pours earrings on us
her teeth are bracelets on the night table

sun moons across the north
moon wanes backwards

here in the antarctic
where nothing is accurate
she/they/we are pierced by sleep

mother shoos a rooster:
'foul-footed you are,
always pestering the poor chooks'

her red face scolding wildly
her wild red face trying to be none the wiser

ungrateful bird she has filled and fed
bird full of apples and worms

sister says he is greedy and not good
selfish like all men and we have held
our tempers too long

shit-spray of fear on the carpet
upside down it seems as tall as she
the heavy bird shaken like a wet lettuce

our red faces laughing wildly
at its gaping affronted beak
our wild red faces trying to be none the wiser

(am I good not greedy
am I important as anyone
am I honey in the crack of the rock)

Mammy Said

An earlier voice, perhaps mine, perhaps the earliest in me,
although the scenario – Isla gets a toy monkey called Bertie
for her birthday – is fictional. I set out to play with
Scottish intonations and rhythms, but Mammy kept butting in
with her forbiddings.

MAMMY SAID YOU KNEEL ON THAT BACK GREEN AGAIN AND
YOU'LL GET ANOTHER SKITE/ LOOK AT THE COLOUR OF YON
KNEES/ IN YOUR BEST DRESS TOO/ CANNY EVEN KEEP YOURSEL
NICE ON YOUR BIRTHDAY/ I SAID I WAS ONLY SHOWING BERTIE
WHAT A BEE WAS LIKE/ FOR IF HE DIDNY KEN/ HE'D MAYBE GO
ON ONE AND HURT HISSEL/ GET A STING LIKE ME/ IT WAS A SORE
YIN ON SCHOOL SPORTS DAY THAT YIN/ BUT I DIDNY GREET/ AND
MISS PATERSON SAID DO YOU LIKE GERMAN BISCUITS ISLA/
HERE'S ONE FOR YOU/ IT HAD WHITE ICING AND HALF A GLASSY
CHERRY ON TOP/ RED JAM IN THE MIDDLE/ I SAID MY DADDY
SHOT GERMANS IN THE WAR/ HE'S GOT A BIG GUN STILL FOR
RABBITS/ SHE PUT A HANKY WI A COLD SMELL ON MY ELBOW/
AND SAID NO TO GO IN FOR THE SACK RACE/ JUST TO SIT BY HER/
AND MAYBE HOLD THE TAPE IF I FELT A WEE BIT BETTER/ I'M
TAKING BERTIE TO SCHOOL AND SHOW HER HIS WAISTCOAT/
AND THE WAY HIS WEE HANDS HANG ON YOUR FINGERS/ I GIED
HIM A FAIRY CAKE TO HOLD BUT IT FELL OUT ON THE RUG/
MAMMY SAID YOU WEE BESOM THE CREAM'LL MARK/ AND
LISBETH THORBURN POKED MAISIE GUNN AND MADE FACES/
BUT I MINDED THAT TIME IN THE LAVVIES WHEN THERE WAS A
MESS IN THE PAN/ AND THEY SAID IT WAS ME/ AND WE'LL TELL
ON YOU/ BUT I DIDNY GREET/ BECAUSE IT WASNY ME/ MY
MAMMY SAID MAISIE GUNN'S MOTHER'S NO RIGHT IN THE
HEID/ SHE GOES WI SAILORS ON THE BIG SHIPS AT DRUMLARIG/
THE RUSSIANS/ THEY'VE GOT RED POMPOMS/ AYE THEY HAVE
AND ALL MY DADDY SAID/ AND MY MAMMY LAUGHED/ MAISIE
GUNN GIED ME NAIL SCISSORS IN A WEE RED CASE/ MAMMY SAID

SHE'LL KEEP THEM IN A DRAWER FOR WHEN I'M BIG/ LIZZIE GIED
ME TRANSFERS/ I'M GOING TO PUT THE FAIRIES IN MY SCHOOL-
BOOK/ AND MOTHER GOOSE TOO/ YOU CAN PUT THEM ON YOUR
ARM/ OR ON YOUR KNEE/ BUT NO ON YOUR SCHOOL SKIRT

The Rothko room, Tate Gallery

Compared to his earlier yellows and
luminous reds, Rothko's late dark
paintings are like barred windows
which refuse the world. There is pity
and empathy here, for the man in the
locked box, but also a rebellion
against his loss of hope, his choice
to make an end of it.

Scarlet let the sun in
under my thumb, but now winter

is truer, maroon has a weight
the air gasps in and out of

I have stopped straining
in bare space

to hear echoes of engines
push the frost to slush

Beyond the window
summer is a blare

At the intersection the dizzy
whites of their clothes

whisk my eyes like eggs
this way and that way

Up out of the subway
people are carrying suitcases

Four black horses rear
against the evening

In the queer sack of illness
I am knifed and safe

So little movement now
except in skies and those

who skid and are bright
on the scarlet crust of the city

My father's plane

When I was a girl
for a while,
I saw my father's plane
cut the light into colours,
make red nights melt
over Dresden,
burn glass and iron.

My father's plane
was only for heroes,
it held me
in its high arms
on sufferance.
I saw others spin down
like sycamores,
like a maypole.

I said I'd not wear breasts
like all women, wait
at the fire
until I was cooked.

Such rainbows we'd ride,
the aviator and I,
hand upon velvet hand.
In our violet oil-slick
we'd slither
through wars, whisper
through gasmasks like lovers:

the future
to the flyer,
the buzzard
to the blood on the road.

in proportion

Many years later, catching
a glimpse of myself,
proper-sized, as if some kind
of restitution had been made. . . .

– it was December
   the wind
   came from the south
   the whole city
   hissed
   a plane dragged
   its sluggish
   diagonal
   through cloud
   drowning
   the horse-voice
   of the chestnut-seller

– the way she laughed, then
   (bending
   over a puddle,
   her long scarf
   swinging scarlet)
   as if a hand
   had moved
   in her life
   or perhaps
   she had run unscathed
   from the scene
   of a disaster,

so that somehow
you knew
for any amount of time
she would find
no fault
in the stars
would be
immune
to all the gloomy moves
of thunder

– just then,
seeing her then,
a woman and a plane
reflected,
a winged pike
swimming in wet leaves
a red scarf
a ripple of fire

Fille de joie

Fille de joie: prostitute, literally,
girl of pleasure. Except that this
girl is pleasure *for herself*, thus the
struggle to admit her. I'm talking
about the muse here.

She enters slantwise, she
is silver in me, I am
at odds with her. She dives
through the V of me
and rises with a butting head

She is beeswax and slippery,
a hot horn when the hedge
hangs green with rain.
When she teases me
with her brushtail and madness
in the drenched circle of leaves
far from punishing I must
learn to seek her widely
in the crook of the cliff
or leaning narrow under
the light in her young parrot noise
and the ravenous night stripes
of her eyes:
> *fille de joie*
> *fille de joie*

postscriptcard

This is where we were
when the moon
nipped at us.
I've marked the bed-
room with a cross.
Believe me,
we were cheap, we were
in heaven, we were
forgetting how to lie.
Wish I was here. Love
Me

accidents of deterioration in which passages are destroyed by rewinding

A rant at the eighties, nihilism, and that moral exhaustion which sees history as no more than a ragbag to be pillaged for Style.

oh glamorous black gloves flirting with microphones
oh hips circling like the stars
oh insignias of irony

oh fishnet and leather prance
oh death dance of heroes
in the shell of the city
oh hoard of history we cannot eat

death
stirs the night hawks
like sex never did
like only leather might
    oh wild scaffold
    oh forgotten ghetto
    oh lovely lovely
in the feathers of yesterday
in the cage of some perhaps city
singing to the sweet sledgehammer
to the smash of the window that breaks us

The Sailor from Gibraltar

A collage, with apologies to Elizabeth
Hardwick's *Sleepless Nights*. Around
these chance phrases of hers, a female
dialogue grew up, a tug of sex and
separation. The title comes from
Marguerite Duras' wonderful ironic
novel of the search for ideal love.

She's looking for a hero,
it's June,
it's a riddle,
this is what she has decided
to do with her life right now

She blooms at the door, birdsong
everywhere,
her soft hiking shoes
shine like copper

Goodbye?
In her dress of printed silk
I applaud her.

Her face is bound tight,
then she might
take out a cigarette:

The weak have the purest sense
of history,
she'll say – Look
at the sailor from Gibraltar,
and that woman with her face
torn by a ship.
I have my wilds to wander
and the seven seas to whore,
What
do you offer?

If only one knew what to remember
or pretend to remember.

Goodbye?
She blooms at the door
in her half-grown-up face,
birdsong everywhere.

She's looking for a hero,
it's June,
it's a riddle,
this is what she has decided
to do with her life right now

Naturally

I expect you'll see her
one day soon
in dappled rain,
naturally,
at the park gates'
or by the canal

Probably you'll carry
a tennis racquet,
and when something says
She's back
you'll ask yourself
who speaks
and marvellously stop seeing
traffic lights and irises

because you'll be watching yourself
wondering
is this me
my steady hand
my slow blue veins
my elaborate arm hanging
naturally

I expect she'll brush past
without touching
your mouth
and you'll ask yourself
is this me
my bucket of bees
my strung bones
frantic with laughter

But you'll be watching yourself
wondering
if the chalk on your tongue
is the sadness
you didn't suck from her

Rodin's Muse

'The soul is transitive: it requires
an object which acts at once as its
direct complement.'   *Francis Ponge*

The Tate Gallery asked various poets
to write about work in their collection.
I brooded around the rooms, feeling
surly and silenced, until I turned
a corner and there she was, Rodin's
Muse, speaking for me, for the
frustration and anger I was trapped
in at that time – frustration of
the artist, the 'seer', but also of the
woman, the 'seen'.

She writhes like hawthorns,
is dark and demented,
her impossibly heavy head
a branch of thoughts the winds
have knotted. In all violence

she loans herself (this muse
who promised him a flat blue
slate to shine his shadow on),
Her calves are rivers
from the glacial snout,

her bruised elbows abut
a space mute and compressing
as rock. The torture starts
not in the lovely torque
of the belly, or even
gravity itself

(this muse who gives no release,
is not delicate, does not dance),
but in a black burning at the pit
of the throat, a capture
of pain and angles somewhere
between his heart and her silence

Jazzsongs for Gina

A student in one of my writing classes
and a fine jazz singer, Gina asked me
for some words to improvise around.
Louis Bird was the name she gave to
her new baby son, in memory of
Charlie 'Bird' Parker.

1. *Moongirls – a Round*

You came in midwinter
through high-angled moonlight
Shaking the fog
from the folds of your coat
I could teach you to quick-
step
Slow slow quick-
step
I could teach you my angles
We could be moongirls at midnight
We could push back the tables
I could teach you to quick-
step
In the frost and the brilliance
Slow slow quick-
step
on the moon dappled floor

2. Louis Bird

little bird he has me
little bird just beginning

little bird in my arms
      my warm arms
little bird in my pool
      my blue pool

little bird he grounds me
little bird just beginning

little bird on no course
      he has me
      he grounds me
and he is flying

3. *November*

November
dust-in-the-eyes days
Draw in deep to your roots
November
dust-in-the-eyes days
Blow and breathe
on your own dark glass
Polish a round
to peer through

November
dust-in-the-eyes days
On the other side of winter
a banned girl dances
bare-armed in sunlight

November
dust-in-the-eyes days
Kiss the wind
with tongues of fire

For Ann, returning

While I was in the Antipodes, Ann was
travelling through South Africa, collect-
ing black women's stories for an anthology.
At a reunion meal she told me some
harrowing tales of her own, but when I
urged her to include these experiences
in the introduction to the book, she
brushed the suggestion aside. 'That's
nothing', she said, 'compared to these
women's lives.'

city night-walking
the moon
bounces along the trees
lights from a balcony
shout of a safer country

I see the long train of Africa
the soldier
daggering the lock
of your compartment door

that cobweb across my mouth
is finger or knife

I shiver like a horse
shadow-horse
cloud of my life racing

'A tender youth without fault or blemish'

'And this was what Findabhair used to say afterwards of any beautiful thing which she saw, that she thought it more beautiful to see Froech across the dark pool; the body so white and the hair so lovely, the face so shapely, the eye so blue, and he a tender youth without fault or blemish, with face narrow below and broad above, and he straight and spotless, and the branch with the red berries between the throat and the white face . . .'

Irish, eighth century, author unknown. From *Táin BóFraich*, translated by Kenneth Hursltone Jackson.

The wings of the mountain
spread out around us
The leagues of the night
move in us, and the moon
with its pale firs,
its black aching rowanberries

The moths
couple like kisses
The woods fall back
to welcome us

In the high ice we burn ourselves
on air and wine

The mouths of mystery exist
and have spoken for us:

A desire unto death.
We draw near and far,
weak-limbed, gigantic

O welcome the flame of the rowan
O welcome our small steps, our long leagues
O welcome the drunk moon and its tongue of tribes

Fantasia for Mary Wollstonecraft

In 1791 when Mary Wollstonecraft wrote her impassioned
Vindication of the Rights of Woman, advocating economic
independence and equal education and civil status as the
preconditions for a free and dignified life for women, she became
the most infamous feminist of her times. 'Women', she wrote,
'may be convenient slaves, but slavery will have its constant
effect degrading the master and the abject dependant.' Mary's
thought was a natural development from the radicalism of
contemporaries like Paine, Condorcet and Godwin – whom she
later married – but the fire and feminism were her own, fuelled
directly by daunting financial and emotional struggles. With
nothing but her wits to live on, she set up a girls' school on
Newington Green – then a hive of Dissidents – and supported her
sisters by teaching, and eventually by writing. Later, when all
revolutionary roads led to France, pregnant by the American
adventurer Gilbert Imlay, she lived through the Terror, observing
the destruction of budding French feminism and completing
(dangerously) her *Historical and Moral View of the French
Revolution*. In 1797, at thirty-nine, she married William Godwin
and died, tragically, of septicaemia in childbirth. Her daughter,
Mary Shelley, was the author of *Frankenstein*.

Mary's free-thinking had its moral and creative rewards, and
also its price – an illegitimate child, bitter disappointments in
love, notoriety, a suicide attempt. But through it all we see the
energy and personality of the woman: impulsive yet tenacious,
imperious yet vulnerable, self-sufficient yet jealous and
demanding – above all, a woman to identify with. Particularly for
me, living here on Newington Green, looking out at the Unitarian
Chapel, imagining her restless and nagging at my shoulder.

There's the same view:
mottled trees, the squat
chapel, the boys
on the spring streets
still raucous
and glossed as blackbirds,

74

yodelling out
for just anybody
and oh
breakneck Mary
how we go round
on the great wheel of April,
to be tugged or broken,
pushed out
still streaked and yolked,
our skin
transparent to the blood

You're here, old bully
at my right ear,
storming radically up
to a broken blue place
where girls will grow
unimaginably into themselves

Your pen leaps across
this blown and blinding day
in the city,
and the dream is
to dare everything – horses,
defeats, vendettas –
to act with a raw edge

Or else you go hungry,
and your thoughts
are the colour of spiders –
that tittering in the distance,
this drab woman
with her schoolmistressy smile,
does she presume?

He's with that actress again,
that pepper-and-salt
rouge-pot, everybody
knows it;
but you don't pine
when your mind is a knife
to slice with –

Into the river, then,
on an oily night without stars,
under the spars of the bridge
your stupid hem
bloating up, blundering yards
of petticoats floating you,
and even your dense energy
won't take you down

Indestructible Mary,
how you sigh
on your dry beach,
the days
sit in your mouth like stones.
Saying you stay alive
only for superior tasks –
all your frippery sisters
just asking to be put in order,
and ardent France, too,
tearing at you like a red
trumpet.

You want fresh strength,
possibilities of men
and mercy and to give
and give, to see love
and revel in the rights
and wrongs of it, to look it
in the teeth. No masks,
now or ever.

Timid Godwin
trembles at your relish –
all this
under the woman's skirts,
desire
silver down her spine,
and doesn't she dance
on his wounds,
teasing and smirking?

The quarrels raking you together,
a stubborn gathering
of two donkeys thinking freely
and biting each other –
so who the devil
would think he'd turn husbandly
and you hold still
and temper
for the child's sake?

Mooning Mary
on a winning streak,
this next birth
will be different.
September-smoky
and encircled by love,
it will be fierce fruit,
a gay
deliverance.
It will give you
Godwin, too, irreversibly.
(This day with the name
of your real death)

Modern Mary
you have travelled
and arrived, yet in the heat
of the heart of it,
a terrible fever
pins you to yourself.
Such ravishing cold –
nothing
was ever meant to be like this

Blackbirds' wings
like a sudden fast scratching,
and even as you
shake your life out
they are using you
singularly
to stifle their girls –

oh shocking
Mary, you strumpet   you
plural woman   you
plainest prophet

Interlude – the windmill

The tower of the mill
turns
on a wheel of kingcups,
yellow heart
of a round table.
In the mirror we are
inside out
like a dog's ear, unprotected
and flushed.

A week away from whispers
we are not quite
strangers;
for listening now we keep
the slatted sails
foursquare
to the stars.

When the door stands
open, all six storeys
billow with wind:
we lean our cheeks against
ice and for once
there is no sensation
of pain

The single woman considers herself

A therapist once said that those people who appear
most independent are in fact the neediest, since
they see their needs and desires as too enormous to
be inflicted on others. . . .

What a hippopotamus love
What a cavern of teeth
What a gobble
What a goat
What a snow-crusted lorry from the far north
What a mire in the handbag
What suitcases of dreams
What packing and unpacking
What a fat orange moon at the end of the night
What a lilac bush bursting in the green air
like God, like a rocket

Below the Ecrins

Ailefroide in the French Alps, and everyone here is
aware of that other country above 10,000 feet:
the glaciers, the curtains and bridges of snow,
the sliced rocks thin as ducks' bills. This is the
frame through which the valley appears so nurturing
and green and safe.

You can be neck-high wet
          in the woods here
where raspberries drip and shine
          Or still
in the shouting field
          where crickets nubbled
and grey as graves
          tick hot time away

Or again, huddled
          in the white window's riot
when the *patron* stops dead, high lightning
          tilting his face like a ship

In the valley there are no strangers.
          Down here
there's the tender twist
          and fuss of flesh,
the luxury of gasps. We shiver,
          knowing what we know.
In the radio burr,
          only the eyes show it

Up there we would be mere pepper
          tossed on the storm
Up there the mountains are pared bare
          by the arbitrary disciplines of heaven

And the clouds are the white flowers
         of the moon
And the seracs are the white teeth
         of the moon

Light bulbs ping
         in the purpling dark. Even
the hands of the card-players
         lose their cunning

Up there you skim clear as a razor
         over your hollowing heart
Your strange heart
         in this blue egg of silence
on the morning you have never been to before

Photographs of the Alps
seen from New South Wales

On the other side
  of the world
where hunched birds
bark and mourn
  and parrots dapple
  the surprising forests
I talk myself
  in and out of them

Somewhere in the back
  of my beyond
is that woman in sunglasses
  a navy-blue intense sky
  gathered, the snow
like nothing you have ever seen:
  white as a whip, blank,
  edible, maddening

I remember you told me
  how crazy gay
you got up there
  sometimes
thinking of throwing yourself
  off.
I could see it, too –
  a jump
  like a shrug,
a faint smile saying
  okay

You with your myths
   and wax,
   working
on the waves of me.
   The exposure
complete: frost fear,
that blue drop

I never thought
   I could fly
   like you,
curve lean and quick
as a missile –
   but what a small ball,
   the Earth,
and as for Europe,
   that lovely dead
   leaf we live on . . .

Somewhere in the back
   of my beyond
   Bahrain
is a flat sand dump
of minarets,
   Singapore
   a bad skid,
electric rain

Let me misplace you.
   Be a witch
offer the apple
or whatever.

Under some black broomstick
   sky
we could always
   annihilate each other –
your hot coasts
my million metaphors for snow

I'm falling
   not landing.
   On some other platform
you are warming your hands,
   12,000 miles ago,
   when the hearts
ran willingly
   out of us

Near that impossible
   edge
   I know
you said
   kiss me. The thrust
   ironic hip,
the ice-axe
   triumphal

Let me take you
   all the way
   from love to slang.
I want to speculate
   on you. Mostly
he wanted a war
   to eat him
but a mountain
   might do.

Honey for nothing.

   Sunspit showers
from nothing but blue
   in this blank land
   my mouth
puzzles at continually

who's been sleeping in my bed?

Sex after celibacy – is there anything it doesn't raise?
Childhood, nurture, mistrust, delight, the Ministry of
Defence. . . .

who's touching me here who's touching you there
whose cats and whose fiddles whose cloud fur
whose bird chatter telling you this telling you
that whose warm bears whose pink dark who's
playing whose pots and whose panhandles whose
perils whose hurdles whose floor skidding with
dry beans who's clumsy who's falling who will
drop who did whose arms whose enemy who's defending
whose daughter who's building the biggest bomb
there is who's bad who's bursting who's no one
who's everyone who's honey who's air who's
for ever?

Rune

Sweet knot of space that the body briefly is
Mouths that all air and kisses enter
The snowstorm, radiant in passing
Wild darkness of all light-filled things